Welcome

This book should help you to make the most of your visit to York Minster. The Minster was built to lift your spirits with devotion and delight and designed as a foretaste of heaven. Look up, because it was designed to be full of light. The result is a series of huge and lovely spaces, changing with every hour of the day. Look around you, too: note the details of the carvings on every pillar and the proportions of the arches and windows. See how the ancient glass lets the sunlight through and changes it. You could visit this place every day for a lifetime and still be noticing new things.

This is a living place, built for daily worship. While you are visiting, there will probably be pauses for prayer. There may well be services in chapels or in the Quire.

Please join us if you wish. Even outside the services themselves there are often events being rehearsed or taking place, because this is a place where things are always going on. Light a candle and say your own prayer.

York Minster is always being renewed and cared for. At present our Great East Window is being restored, and you may well see other work going on in other parts of the building. We hope this will add to the pleasure and interest of your visit, as you see the skilled work going on, and the improvements being made to the Minster for the enjoyment of our visitors.

Visit slowly. And often, in the years to come, think of us.

Keith Jones

The Very Reverend Keith Jones, Dean of York

Light reflected onto the South Transept ceiling from the Rose Window.

Contents

York Minster

'This is a living place, built for daily worship.'

Introduction

York Minster, like many other churches, is a building that tells a story. The story it tells, in stone and glass, architecture and layout, is the story of the Christian faith. That's what it was built for. It was also built to be an expression on earth of the Kingdom of Heaven, of the power of the Church and of those who built it. It was built to be a place of remembrance, celebration, and above all prayer. Whatever the motivations of those who built and endowed it, and of those who come to visit, York Minster is and remains a holy place – a place of prayer and pilgrimage for over 1,300 years.

The Journey from West to East

The Great West Doors are the ceremonial entrance to the Minster, used by archbishops when they begin their ministry and used by royalty when they visit. From here you get a sense of the scale of the building and from here you can also 'read' it all.

Outside the doors, at least symbolically, there is danger and darkness; the chaos and disorder of a sinful world. Inside the building is light and safety; the dignity and order of the Kingdom of God. The glass and the decoration of the building you enter creates a dazzling world of colour and light.

Far left: York Minster from the City walls.
Left: Nave roof detail.
Above: statue of an archbishop
over the West Doors.
Above right: statues of the Apostles
at the West End.
Right: King Manasseh from the Jesse
Window in the South Quire Aisle.

The building is designed to work from the west to the east, telling the story of salvation. The main roof bosses of the Nave ceiling – the ones with a light blue background – tell of the 'Joys of Mary' and some of the main events in the life of Jesus. Near the Great West Doors we see Mary being told that she will have a baby (the Annunciation); near the middle we see the Ascension of Jesus (look for the soles of his feet) and by the Central Tower we see Mary's coronation as Queen of Heaven. The Nave is a sort of 'ceremonial way' leading you along the path of salvation; a way lined with the stories from the Bible, the lives of the saints, and the deeds of faithful Christian people (including those who donated the windows); a crowd urging you on towards holiness and faith.

As you arrive under the Central Tower at the Quire Screen with its carvings of secular kings, you then ascend through the Quire into the holier spaces until you reach the High Altar; the very gateway of Heaven where Christ himself feeds and prepares us. Standing above it all is the Great East Window with its summary of everything: the beginning and the end with God the Father at the very top, the origin and goal of all things.

Detail of a Norman
column in the crypt.

Below: the Lady Chapel and Quire ceiling.
Right: a view of York from the Central Tower.

Above: Tim Foster carving a grotesque.
Right: Choristers singing.
Far right: 'Madness' carved by Matthew Hodgkinson.

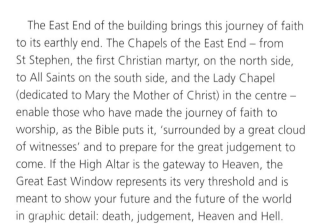

The East End of the building brings this journey of faith to its earthly end. The Chapels of the East End – from St Stephen, the first Christian martyr, on the north side, to All Saints on the south side, and the Lady Chapel (dedicated to Mary the Mother of Christ) in the centre – enable those who have made the journey of faith to worship, as the Bible puts it, 'surrounded by a great cloud of witnesses' and to prepare for the great judgement to come. If the High Altar is the gateway to Heaven, the Great East Window represents its very threshold and is meant to show your future and the future of the world in graphic detail: death, judgement, Heaven and Hell.

The Guidebook

Elsewhere in this book you can read about the huge restoration project York Minster is currently undertaking on the stone and the glass of the East End, and there are displays in the Chapels of the East End to help you understand what is happening. You will also find more detail about the different areas of the Minster, so you can use this book to find your way around and to see some parts that aren't normally open to visitors.

You might also like to take time to visit the area around the Minster where there is more to see.

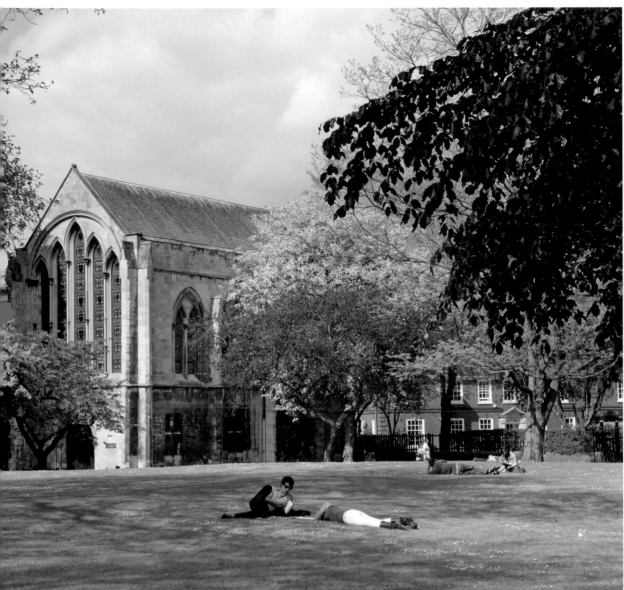

Left: the Old Palace
and Dean's Park
Above: the interior
of the Old Palace.

On the north side you will find Dean's Park, one of the largest green spaces in the city. On the edge of Dean's Park there is The Old Palace – the office of the Collections Manager and home of the Minster's Historic Collections, the Library, and the Archives and Modern Records. There are often exhibitions held there. Near the East End you will find St William's College, medieval home of the chantry priests who worked in the Minster, and the Masons' Lodge, a working recreation of the way the masons who built York Minster did their job. Near the Roman Column outside the south side of the Minster is the Minster School, where the Minster's choristers and about 120 other children receive their education up to 13 years of age.

Towards the back of this guidebook there is a substantial glossary of terms to do with architecture, the Church and history which you might find helpful in using the book. It can also be helpful to remember that this Church, like many others, is built so that the High Altar in the Quire is in the east. It is easiest to point things out by giving a direction, so if you can remember that looking towards the High Altar is to the east you should be able to locate things mentioned in the book wherever you are.

- Built between 1291 and the 1350s in the Decorated Gothic style.

- Length 264 ft (80 m); width 100 ft (30 m); height from floor to vaulting 94 ft (29 m).

- In 1840 the Nave roof and belfry were completely destroyed by a fire started accidentally when a clockmaker left a candle burning.

- York's Nave is one of the longest in England.

- The Great West Window cost £67 to create and install in 1338.

- The Nave has only been used for services since 1863. Many concerts and events also take place in this space.

The Nave

The pillars in the Nave mark the line of the outside walls of the Norman cathedral. Many of the statues in the Nave have no heads as a result of damage during the Reformation.

Left: St Peter.
Top: the Nave looking east.
Above: the Nativity boss
(note the baby Jesus being
bottle-fed).
Right: the Altar cross with
the West Window, known as
the Heart of Yorkshire.

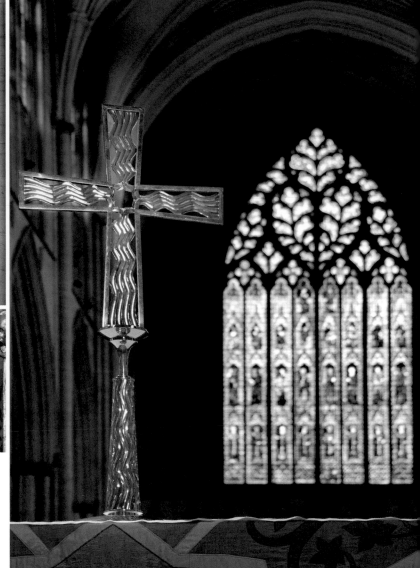

The Nave

The main body of the Minster, the Nave (from the Latin word *navis* meaning 'ship', because of its shape), is the widest Gothic Nave in England. The width of the main roof was too great to span in stone so it is made of wood. On the walls above its arches are the shields of the nobles who accompanied Edward I on his campaigns against the Scots at the end of the 1200s, and in the glass of the clerestory windows (the highest level of windows) above are those who came later with Edward II in the early 1300s. Also in the clerestory are several panels of Norman glass that survive from the earlier Minsters, 'recycled' to save money in the 1300s.

Several of the large windows of the Nave were glazed at the expense of donors who had themselves incorporated into the design and who possibly also paid for Masses at the associated chantry altars which were once all around the Nave in the medieval period. One notable example is Richard Tunnoc, a bell founder and Mayor of York who died in 1330, who is depicted praying to St William in a window otherwise filled with symbols and depictions of the making

The Dragon's Head.

10

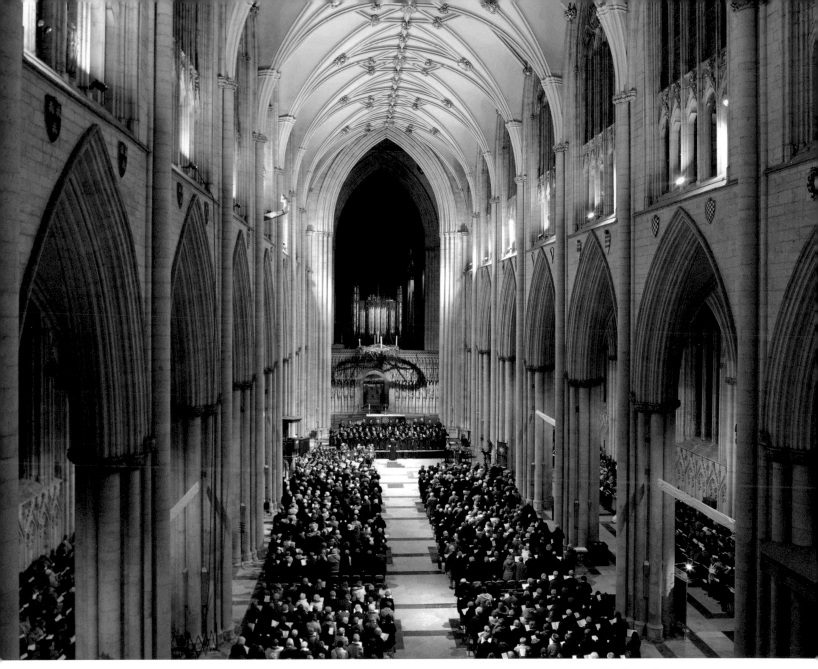

The Minster Carol Concert.

of bells (north side, second to the west of St John's Chapel). Sticking out from the triforium arcading at about the mid-point of the north side is the famous dragon's head. This is thought to be the remains of an elaborate lifting mechanism for raising, by way of a chain through the dragon's neck, either the 50 ft (15.2 m) high cover known to have adorned the medieval font, but lost at the Reformation, or even the cover for a significant reliquary. The dragon is made of solid oak. It would take at least a couple of strong people to make it work (it's in the 'up' position). The present font, kept in St Cuthbert's Chapel at the west end of the south side, is a movable one made by

Charles Gurrey in 2003 and paid for by the Friends of York Minster. It is made of sycamore and bronze, incorporating a fish, the earliest Christian symbol, and the water of life.

The Nave roof, including the medieval roof bosses, was completely destroyed by fire in 1840. All of the eight key roof bosses, each about 3 ft (1 m) across and with a blue background, which portray the life of Christ and the Blessed Virgin Mary, were replaced with exact replicas except the Nativity boss (second from the west end); Victorian sensibilities demanded that the Virgin should be depicted bottle-feeding the infant Christ instead of breastfeeding.

The Great West Window, known as 'the heart of
Yorkshire' because of the shape formed by the stonework
of the upper part, was built in 1338–9 by Master Mason
Ivo de Raghton and was glazed by Master Richard
Ketelbarn under the direction of Archbishop Melton.
It illustrates the authority and purpose of the Church
in the form of a hierarchy going up the window. The
bottom row contains eight Archbishops of York, including
Melton, above which are the Apostles from whom the
archbishops derive their authority. Above them are four
pairs of panels depicting the life of Christ and the Virgin –
the Annunciation, Nativity, Resurrection and Ascension –

Right: the Assumption boss.

The Nave looking west.

and finally, above it all, is a scene set in Heaven showing Mary crowned as Queen, sitting at the side of Christ. The stonework of the window had to be completely replaced in 1989–90, due the effects of pollution and erosion, and the carved outside arches of the doorway beneath the window were replaced in 1998. These include one row which is a new carved interpretation of the events of the Book of Genesis, to a design by Rory Young. Created by the Minster's carvers, the figurative stones are carved beneath canopies where the artistry and imagination of the carvers themselves have been given full reign, following centuries of tradition. The continuous work of

maintenance on the Minster ensures that the traditional skills are not only kept alive but allowed to flourish, and that the Minster continues to evolve as each age makes its contribution.

At the other end of the Nave, you can see the organ above the *pulpitum*; the Quire or Kings' Screen. The organ was entirely replaced after a fire in 1829, and has been restored and maintained many times since. It has over 5,300 pipes. It is clear from the archives that an organ of some sort has been used in the Minster since at least the 1300s, and in the 1700s there were several, including at least one 'great organ', probably in the Quire.

Above: carving of a knight fighting a wild animal, over the south-west door.
Right: detail of the Nave roof bosses.
Far right: the organ.

The organ has not always been on top of the screen; in 1631 the Dean and Chapter applied to the Crown to use a £1,000 fine they had received towards a new organ and this was installed in 1634 but, at the request of Charles I, it was placed on the north side of the Quire, where it would not obstruct the view of the Great East Window from the Nave. This was completely destroyed during the English Civil War, so that no trace remained. Following the Restoration in 1660, plans were immediately put into effect to restore an organ to the Minster, and certainly there was one in use again by 1666. By 1688 it was in its present position on the screen, where it is in daily use for services

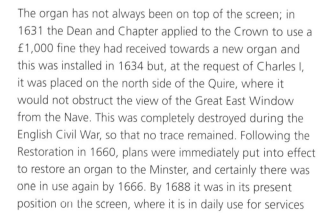

A carving of a wife beating her husband.

14

Richard Tunnoc, donor of the Bell-Founder's Window.

and is frequently used for recitals and concerts by organists from all over the world.

After the Reformation swept away the altars and shrines of the medieval Minster, the Nave was left largely bare. It was filled during the Commonwealth period (mid 1600s) with York citizens who flocked to hear the preachers and to sing psalms, but during the 1700s and 1800s it was primarily a secular space where local gentry could enjoy a stroll in the dry or listen to a concert. The Nave had no seating except the stone sills around the walls until the 1860s, when Dean Duncombe introduced benches to encourage attendance at services 'by the labouring classes'.

Before that, all services other than major processions were held in the Quire. Today the Nave is in use weekly for Sunday services, and is filled regularly with people attending one of the many services held for a wide variety of groups and organisations. Seating around 2,000 people, it is also a venue for concerts and other large events, where the Christian community in the north of England and the city of York can gather for prayer, commemoration and celebration.

God's presence is truly here

A visitor, England

- Built between 1220 and c.1253 in the Early English, or First Period Gothic, style.

- Length 223 ft (68 m); width of Transepts 95 ft (29 m); height of Central Tower internally 184 ft (56 m).

- The South Transept roof was destroyed after a lightning storm caused a fire on 9 July 1984.

- The windows in the Central Tower are the same height as the Five Sisters Window.

- Charles Dickens' book, *Nicholas Nickleby*, features the legend of how the Five Sisters Window was created.

- The Undercroft was created as a result of strengthening the Tower between 1967 and 1972.

The Transepts and Tower

The Transepts and Tower create the arms of the cross.

In the Transepts you can see evidence of the Norman building.

South Transept

The South Transept is the earliest part of the present building. Begun in 1220, it was largely the vision of Archbishop Walter de Gray whose tomb, made of Purbeck marble and limestone, can be seen on the east side, with its effigy and elaborate canopy. The style of rounded, complex arches used by de Gray in the arcading above you is quite different from the pointed, simpler arches below and show that he was building at a point of transition from one style to another. The South Transept entrance was originally

Detail of the crucifix in the South Transept.

conceived as one of the great processional spaces, linking the Minster with the city along Stonegate to the Guildhall and the river. Above the door, at the top of the south wall, is the famous Rose Window. Its stonework, dating from 1240, contains later glass from the early 1500s, representing the red Lancaster and Tudor roses from which its modern name derives. It was re-glazed to mark the union of the Houses of York and Lancaster under Henry VII. Damaged in the fire of 1984,

Two of the 'Blue Peter' bosses;
the Tudor rose in flames and
'Saving the Whale'.

which destroyed the roof, the restored window was called the Marigold Window for many years, reflecting the shape of the tracery, before the term Rose Window was coined. The restored roof of 1988 has 68 colourful bosses, depicting the words of the *Benedicite*, the ancient Biblical hymn of praise. It has recently inspired the York Minster Rose, a bed of which has been planted in the Dean's Park near the west end of the Minster.

We had to recreate a masterpiece

Bob Littlewood, Clerk of Works, on the restoration after the 1984 fire

Above: The Assumption of Mary in the archway of the Quire screen.

Quire Screen

Also known as the Kings' Screen or the *pulpitum*, the stone screen that forms the western entrance to the Quire is one of the most famous parts of the Minster. It is carved with 15 large statues of the kings of England, from William the Conqueror to Henry VI – those who were on the throne during York Minster's Norman and Gothic phases. The screen is unusual in being asymmetrical, with the doorway off-centre, seven statues to the north and eight to the south. The most likely explanation is that the substantial screen was originally designed around 1420 as part of the engineering work to strengthen the arches of the eastern end following a tower collapse in 1407. The intention was

to have 14 statues of the kings up to Henry V, but his unexpectedly short reign (1413–22) meant a hasty revision was needed in order to include a statue of Henry VI, who was crowned before it was finished. After Henry VI was murdered, his statue apparently attracted 'improper reverence' and was removed and replaced several times (including once with a statue of James I, now in Ripon Cathedral), before finally being replaced with the present statue by Michael Taylor in 1810. This statue is smaller than the others and in a notably different style. Traces of the original paint that once made these statues brightly coloured can still be seen.

Above: the south side of the Quire Screen.
Below: Edward III.

The design is extraordinary in that the doorway is not central, having seven niches for statues on the north and eight on the south

John H. Harvey, 1977

An idea of what they might have looked like can be found by looking up at the beautiful roof boss of the Assumption of the Virgin from the early 1400s in the vault of the doorway into the Quire. Above the kings is a row of angels playing courtly musical instruments and above that, near the top of the screen, a frieze of more prosaic angels playing instruments such as Northumbrian pipes, 'serpents' and sackbuts.

The Tower

The Central Tower of York Minster is the only part of the present building to have the same 'footprint' as its Norman predecessor; everything else has been enlarged. The Tower's present size and shape is not, however, what was originally planned. It was supposed to have an upper level with bells, and was probably to be topped off with a spire. This is the only part of the Minster to have collapsed (in 1407), and when you look at the walls around the Tower you can see the distortion in some of the stonework that gives you an idea of the enormous strain it was under from the present Tower. Thanks to major works in the early 1970s the Tower is now stable. To give you some sense of

scale, the windows in the upper part of the Tower are the same height as the Five Sisters Window in the North Transept.

Just above the arches formed by the bottom part of the Tower there are four pairs of coats of arms. As you face the east side, over the Quire Screen, to your left, on the north side are the arms of the Ancient See of York; to your right, on the south side are the arms of St Wilfrid. On the south side of the Tower, looking towards the South Transept, to your left, on the east side, are the arms of St Peter which have a defaced Papal Tiara at the top, and, on your right, on the west side the arms of Bishop Walter Skirlaw of

Durham (d. 1406) who paid for the Great East Window and much of the Central Tower. On the west side of the Tower, looking back down the Nave there are, on your left, on the south side, the arms of Henry IV (d. 1413) who sent his Master Mason to help build the Tower and, on your right, on the north side, the arms of Edward the Confessor (d. 1066). On the north side of the Tower, facing the North Transept are, on your left, on the west side, the arms of King Edwin of Northumbria (d. 633) whose baptism led to the founding of York Minster and, on your right, on the east side, the arms of King Oswald of Northumbria (d. 642) who built the first stone Minster.

At the very top, in the centre of the ceiling of the Central Tower, is a massive roof boss showing Saints Peter and Paul. Saint Peter is holding York Minster in his hand. If you look carefully you can see a cable hanging down from alongside the Peter and Paul roof boss. This cable is used a couple of times a year; to hang the massive Advent Wreath with its five large candles from Advent Sunday through to the end of the Christmas period, and a large wooden Cross from Good Friday through to the end of the Easter period.

Makes you proud to be from Yorkshire

A visitor

North Transept

The Five Sisters Window dominates the North Transept and characterises its austere beauty. Built in the mid 1200s, largely at the expense of the Sub-Dean, John Romanus, the North Transept's architecture is what has come to be called Early English. The window is filled with *grisaille* glass (from the French for 'greyness'); finely-painted, clear glass set into geometric designs with jewel-like points of coloured glass making the pattern. The more colourful panel of the Old Testament Prophet Habakkuk inserted into the centre of the bottom row of the window is much earlier glass, c.1150, taken from the Norman Minster. The Women's Screen, a memorial to the women of the Empire who died

Above: St John's Chapel.
Right: details from the Astronomical Clock.

Above: The Astronomical Clock.
Right: The Five Sisters Window.

serving in World War I, separates the St Nicholas Chapel on the east side from the Astronomical Clock – a memorial to the Allied aircrews who flew from airbases in Yorkshire and the North-East and lost their lives in World War II. On one face of the Clock is shown the precise position of the sun in relation to the Minster at any time, and on the other the position of the northern stars, by which aircrew navigated at night. Dedicated in 1955, the memorial also contains a Book of Remembrance. Today the North Transept is also often used as a space for exhibitions.

A detail of the left-hand light of the Five Sisters Window.

The middle chapel, now known as St Nicholas Chapel, is said on very slight authority to have been that of St Thomas of Canterbury

Minster Guidebook, 1930

- Built between c.1260 and 1286 in the Decorated Gothic style.

- Diameter 63 ft (19 m); height to top of the vault 66 ft (20 m).

- Edward I's Parliament was held in the Chapter House in 1297.

- Some of the medieval painted panels which originally decorated the ceiling are now part of the Historic Collection.

- The Chapter House Vestibule contains some of the earliest figurative glass, still in its original location, in York Minster.

- The Masons' Loft is the location of York Minster's oldest indoor toilet.

The Chapter House

One of the Minster's hidden delights, the Chapter House is accessed from the eastern corner of the North Transept, but is concealed from view by its Vestibule, itself an architectural jewel.

Left: the entrance to the Chapter House.
Above: one of the many carvings in the canopies.
Right: the Chapter House roof.

The Chapter House, Chapter House Roof and the Vestibule

Completed and in use by 1286, the octagonal Chapter House is unusual in not having a central column to support the great vaulted ceiling. Instead the weight of the ceiling is suspended from the roof above. This was unique at the time of its construction, and there is a model to show the complex engineering used to hold up the ceiling and to spread the load created by the timbers in the roof.

Above the Vestibule is the Masons' Loft. This was the space used by the Master Mason to draw out the patterns for the templates used by the masons to build parts of the Minster. We can still see the last drawings he made before the Loft was no longer used in the early 1400s. Wooden

templates from the 1800s, and later metal templates, are still stored there. It is also the location of the oldest indoor toilet in the Minster. You can find out about visiting the Chapter House Roof and the Masons' Loft on one of the 'Hidden Tours' by looking on the Minster's website (www.yorkminster.org) or by ringing the information number in this book.

Just before you enter the Chapter House look high up on the right-hand (south) wall and you can see some remnants of the original decoration scheme of the Vestibule.

Soon after its completion, from the 1290s onwards, the Chapter House was used for Parliaments by Edward I and

Left: detail of markings on the floor of the Masons' Loft.
Below left: a carving of the Virgin and Child in the doorway.
Below: the Masons' Loft.

Edward II during their campaigns against the Scots. It is still used as a meeting place a few times a year for meetings of the College of Canons and as a place for part of the installation of new canons. Around the walls are the 44 seats of the College. Each canon has an equal voice in these meetings, and the Dean is seen as 'first amongst equals', so the seats are arranged in groups of six, making it impossible for the Dean to sit in a central seat. Some of the Minster's finest carvings are to be found around the canopies of these seats: a wonderful collection of the faces, hair styles and hats of the people of York, funny faces, animals and mythical beasts. Around 80 per cent are original carvings from 1270–80 and the remainder were carved by George Peter White during the 1845 Beckwith restoration of the Chapter House. This restoration which, sadly, saw the walls largely scrubbed clean of their remaining wall paintings, also installed the Minton tile floor with its design based on the patterns in the windows.

As the rose is the
flower of flowers,
so this is the
house of houses

Undated medieval inscription in the doorway of the Chapter House

- Built between 1361 and 1472 in the Perpendicular Gothic style.

- Length (including East End) 224 ft (68 m); width 105 ft (32 m); height 101 ft (31 m).

- The only royal burial in York Minster is Prince William of Hatfield, whose parents Edward III and Philippa of Hainault, married here in 1328. William's tomb is in the North Quire Aisle.

- In 1829 Jonathan Martin deliberately set fire to the Quire, destroying the vaulting and wooden stalls.

- In the South Quire Aisle there is a memorial to Jane Hodson who gave birth to 24 children before dying at the age of 38.

The Quire and East End

The Quire represents a 'church within a church'.

Most sung services are held in the Quire.

From left to right: detail of vaulting in the Savage Tomb; figure holding a shield on the tomb of Archbishop Savage; detail of a figure carved on the arcading of the wall. Above: roof vaulting in the North Quire Aisle.

North Quire Aisle

The North Quire Aisle contains the Minster's only royal tomb, a reconstructed chantry chapel, and the stunning St William Window. The tomb of Prince William of Hatfield, son of Edward III, has been situated in several places around the Minster, but was returned to what is thought to be its original location, at the west end near the North Transept, in 1979. The figure is that of a young boy, but William actually died as a baby, aged about four months, in 1337. The canopied niche was repainted with the design of red and gold broom twigs, the badge of the Plantagenets, in the 1980s, and was based on original paint traces found on the stone. To the east of the tomb, on the same side

A panel from the St William Window showing a lame woman at the shrine.

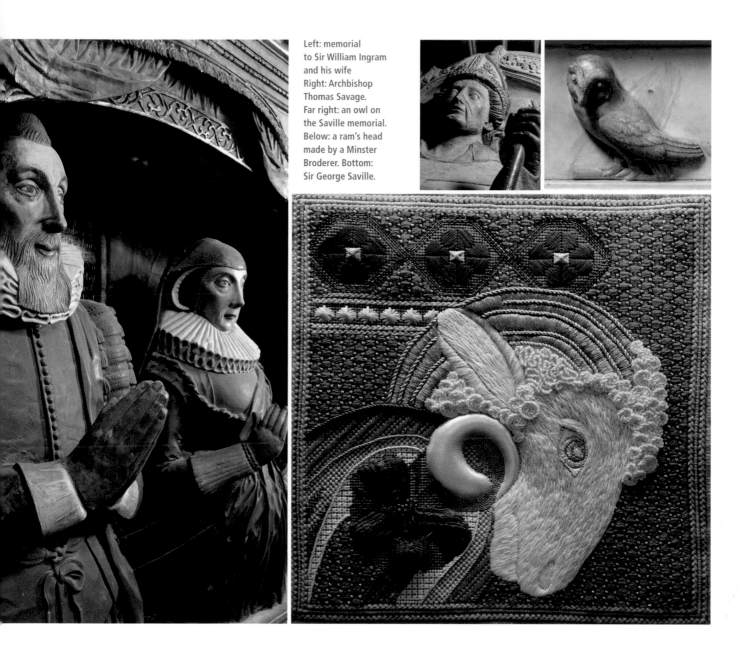

and just along from the door leading to the toilets, is the soaring St William Window, which, like the Great East Window, was made by John Thornton and dates from the early 1400s. The window shows scenes from the life and miracles of Archbishop William Fitzherbert, who died in 1154. Fitzherbert was canonised (made a Saint) in 1227 and his shrine became a great place for pilgrims, including Edward II who carried a bone of St William in his personal collection of relics. On the south side of the aisle, opposite the St William Window and attached to the Quire, is the tomb of Archbishop Thomas Savage, who died in 1507. The tomb has a reconstructed chantry chapel above it. There were once about 60 such chapels in the medieval Minster, attended by up to 20 chantry priests who sang Masses for the souls of the dead. The chapels and the priests were swept away in the Reformation of the 1500s. This chantry was chosen to be rebuilt because it was also used as a watch tower for the Shrine of St William, when it was located where the present High Altar now stands.

> The chief beauty of the aisles of the Quire is the glass in the windows… amongst the finest glass in the Minster

Minster Guidebook, 1930

Above: the Minster organ.
Left: an angel on the organ case.
Top left: choristers singing.

Quire

As with many cathedrals, York has a Quire enclosed by screens. The Quire is where services are traditionally sung and where the Archbishop of York has his special seat or *cathedra* (halfway along on the south side). Along the sides are the stalls of the canons, each with its badge or plaque showing the 'prebend' to which the canonry belongs. A 'prebend' was the estate from which the canons received their income. All the original woodwork, the roof, and some of the stonework of the Quire was destroyed in a fire in 1829, which was started by a man called Jonathan Martin. The restoration is a 'free copy' because there were no detailed drawings, unlike for the roof bosses in the Nave when they were restored after the fire in 1840. The only major omission was the decision not to recreate

...a faire large high Organ, newly built richly gilt, carv'd & painted & a sweet snowy Crew of singers   Capt. Hammond, 1634

Above: the Quire.
Below: Evensong taking place in the Quire.

the 'misericords' (carvings found underneath the seats), but instead to put in the fixed seats that are there today. High above on the walls between the arches are shields and coats of arms of those who originally helped to fund the building of the Minster in the Middle Ages; higher still are the windows from the 1300s with their great figures of saints and kings. It is in the Quire that Evensong is sung most days by the choir of the Minster or by one of the many visiting choirs who sing during the holidays. York Minster was one of the earliest English Cathedrals to have girls as well as boys in the choir.

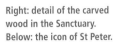

Right: detail of the carved
wood in the Sanctuary.
Below: the icon of St Peter.

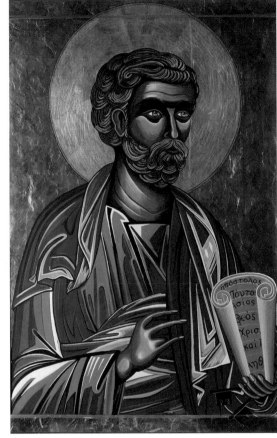

The Thompson mouse above the
Dean's stall in the Sanctuary.

High Altar

The High Altar stands more than 6.5 ft (2 m) above the level
of the Nave: it is physically and spiritually the high point of
the Minster. Once, this area would have been dominated by
the shrine of St William, whose tomb is now in the crypt
below the Quire. The High Altar is the *sanctum sanctorum*
or 'Holy of Holies' and is the focal point of the Quire.

...the childish recollection of the service
has not faded away, but has ever mingled
with the most inspiring thoughts
of the public worship of God

Harvey Goodwin, Church Congress Report, 1866

The Quire and High Altar.

The Altar, with the cross on top, is a reminder to Christians of what Jesus did to open up a new relationship to God and it is central to worship in the Church. The colours of the altar cloths, or frontals, here as elsewhere in the Minster, are changed according to the season in the Church's year; they vary from richly embroidered white and gold for festivals such as Christmas and Easter to solemn blues and purples for the penitential seasons of Advent and Lent. The large and richly coloured carpet in front of the Altar is one of a number of Persian and Middle Eastern rugs and carpets, collected by Dean Milner-White (Dean from 1941 to 1963) to adorn the Minster. Unlike the

woodwork of the Quire, which dates from the 1830s, the stalls in the sanctuary area around the High Altar are the work of the woodcarver 'Mousey' Thompson from Kilburn in North Yorkshire and were carved in the early 1940s. His signature, a small wooden mouse, is carved on some of his pieces and there are several examples around the Minster (though not everywhere, since the Dean at the time didn't want too many church mice in the building!). There are two statues on either side of the High Altar: on the north side King Edwin, whose baptism in 627 took place in the first Minster Church and, on the south side Edward VII, who died in 1910.

Below: the urn on top of Archbishop
Lamplugh's memorial.
Bottom: the Minster banner.
Right: a weeping cherub on the
Wentworth memorial in All Saints' Chapel.

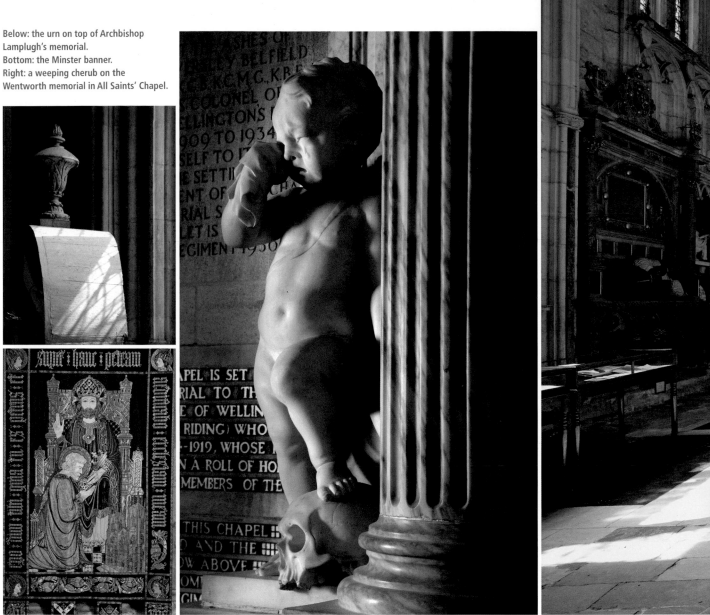

South Quire Aisle

On the south wall, near to the South Transept, is the
Great Processional Banner, showing the crucifixion on one
side and Christ giving St Peter the keys to the Kingdom
of Heaven on the other. Made in the 1920s, it is carried in
procession at major services. At this end of the South Quire
Aisle you can also see some of the pipes from the organ,
including the great 32 ft (9.8 m) pipe, and the 'brain'
which controls the Minster's sound system. Further along
the Aisle on the north side, and attached to the Quire,
are two cases containing the delicate crystal primatial
cross of the Archbishop of York and the Minster's gilded
processional cross. Set into the panelling, also on the

north side, is the curious polished wood memorial to
members of the Gale family. Made in 1963, it incorporates
a jester's head and two coats of arms, which once formed
the lid of an older chest from the household of the Gale

family. George Gale was
Mayor of York in 1556
and his descendant,
Thomas, was Dean of
York in 1702. On the
south side, opposite the
Gale memorial, are two
doors: the double door

Anna Bennett in All Saints' Chapel.

The South Quire Aisle with the cope chests
and the memorial to Archbishop John Dolben.

towards the East End is the entrance to the Zouche Chapel, reserved for private prayer; the other, over which there are two bells, is the Vestry where the vergers prepare for services. On the north side, next to the steps into the Eastern Crypt, are two medieval cope chests, in which were once stored flat the heavily jewelled and embroidered cape-like robes of the clergy, worn in great processional services. Further towards the East End, on the floor just outside All Saints' Chapel is a floor slab, divided by the

wrought iron screen of the chapel. It is the cover to the family vault of the Earl of Strafford. It is the final resting place of the only British Prime Minister buried in York Minster, Lord Rockingham, who was Prime Minister twice: first in 1765–66 (followed by William Pitt the Elder) and briefly in 1782. It was in 1782 that Rockingham formally acknowledged the independence of the American colonies just before his death. The Treaty of Paris which formalised this was signed in September 1783.

…by the aire and mien he looks more like a soldier or a Beau than a Bishop, and so it seems he was in humour

Diary of Celia Fiennes, 1685, on Archbishop Lamplugh's memorial

41

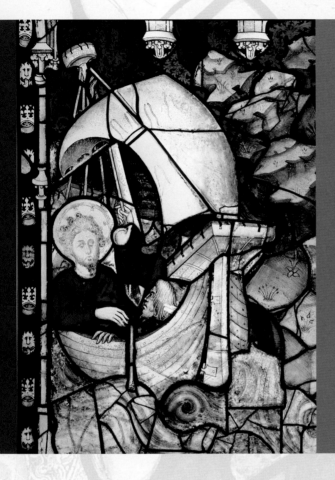

- The Lady Chapel was the location of the 12.30 pm Holy Communion service until the scaffolding was erected in 2008.

- There are 16 miles (26 km) of scaffolding around the East End exterior at the moment.

- The *King's Book of Heroes* is housed in All Saints' Chapel. The book contains the names of all the soldiers from York who died in the Great War of 1914–18.

- The East End is the resting place for a number of archbishops. The most recent to be interred here was Archbishop Garbett who died in 1955.

The East End

The East End of the Minster is undergoing a major restoration project called York Minster Revealed. This section of the book explores the project.

Above: St John arrives on the Island of Patmos.
Facing page: the army of horsemen.
Both from the Revelation sequence of the Great East Window.

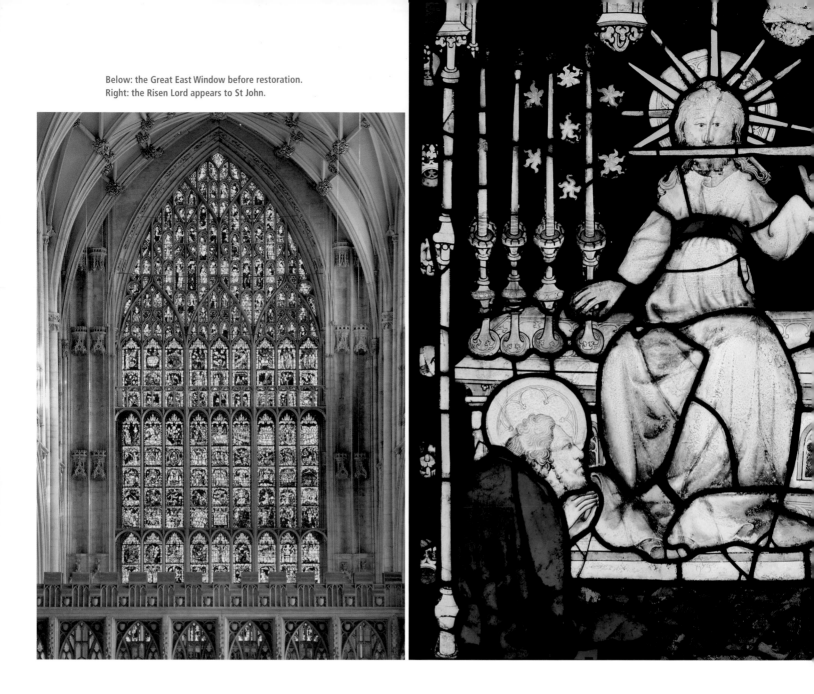

Below: the Great East Window before restoration.
Right: the Risen Lord appears to St John.

The East End

At present the East End contains information about the conservation and restoration of the stained glass of the Great East Window in St Stephen's Chapel on the north side; about the conservation and restoration of the stonework in All Saints' Chapel on the south side, and about the Great East Window and its maker, John Thornton, in the Lady Chapel in the centre. You can see the masons at work in the Masons' Lodge outside the East End of the Minster, and there are tours of the Bedern Chapel to see the York Glaziers' Trust at work on the Great East Window. More information about both can be found on www.yorkminster.org. There is more information about the chapels later on in this guidebook.

Great East Window

The glory of the East End of the Minster is undoubtedly the Great East Window. Today, as the window undergoes a major programme of conservation and restoration, its place is taken by the world's highest resolution digital graphic of the window, which is nearly life-size. It was made by EPS of Leeds and hung in 2008. The Great East Window was made between 1405 and 1408 by John Thornton of Coventry, the foremost master glazier of his day, and his workshop. This is one of the finest, and the largest, medieval stained glass windows in the world. Larger than a tennis court, it contains 117 panels in rows of nine,

Far left: detail of a dog.
Left: three gossiping angels.
Above: the message to the Seven Churches.
Top right: the Lamb takes the book.
Right: detail of the Elders wearing their crowns.

in addition to the tracery at the top. The panels towards the upper middle of the window, below the small tracery panels, depict the seven days of Creation and events of the Hebrew Bible and, in the two sections of panels below, a graphic representation of the Book of Revelation, the last book of the Bible. It was intended to make the worshipper think about of the health of their soul and to show the judgements to come. At the very top of the window, almost hidden within the tracery, is the figure of God with the words *Ego sum Alpha et Omega* – 'I am the Alpha and the Omega, the beginning and the end'. Copies of the Dean and Chapter's contract with Thornton survive, which show he was paid £56 by Walter Skirlaw, Bishop of Durham, who is shown in the window. Thornton received a £10 bonus for finishing on time, but according to his contract had risked being paid nothing if the Dean and Chapter didn't like the finished window. There is more information about the window, John Thornton and the restoration programme in the Lady Chapel.

One of the faces painted by John Thornton, before restoration.

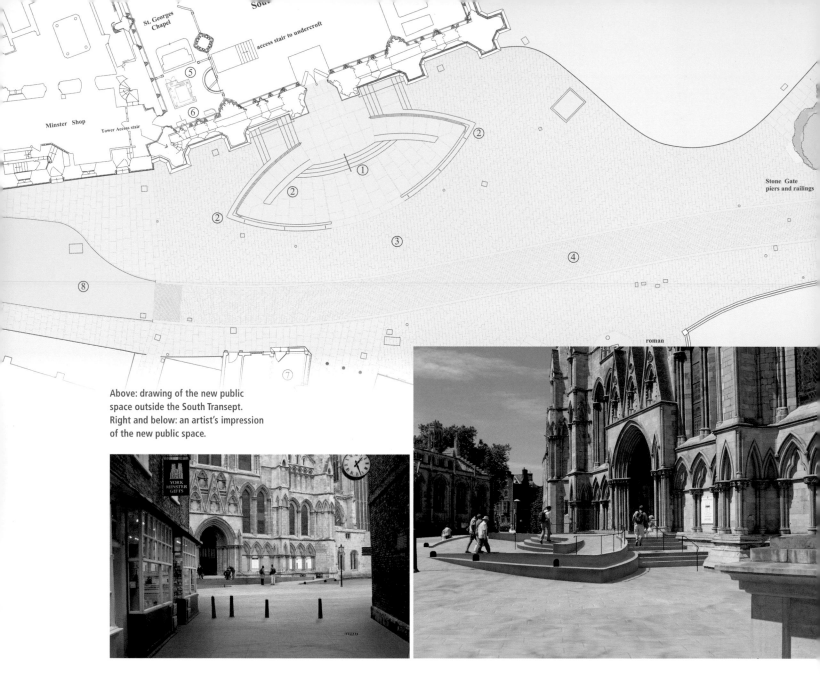

Above: drawing of the new public space outside the South Transept. Right and below: an artist's impression of the new public space.

York Minster Revealed

The York Minster Revealed (YMR) Project is one of the biggest conservation projects ever undertaken by York Minster. The Project is made up of a number of parts. The centrepiece is the conservation and restoration of the stonework of the East End and just over half of the glass of the Great East Window. The Great East Window is one of the great masterpieces of visual art in England and the YMR Project aims to make it easier to see and to understand and to make it safe for generations to come. Also, the Project is working to make easier access to the Minster from outside, better access to the Undercroft Museum and Crypts, and improved facilities for visitors, such as more toilets. During the time of the YMR Project

there will be scaffolding covering the outside of the East End and the whole of the Great East Window inside. This means that the Chapels of the East End are not in use for worship until the project is complete.

Ease of physical access into and around the Minster is a principal aim of the YMR Project. Outside the main visitor entrance to the Minster there will be a new public space for the city with an elegant double ramp to welcome everyone through the same door. Ticketing for entrance to the Minster will be moved out of the building and into the shops opposite the south door. The whole area will be paved to make it a more attractive and useable space; a gathering point for the city.

Left: the Masons' Lodge.
Top: the Stoneyard with
stone to be worked.
Above: a Minster carver
working on the stone.
Right: scaffolding
covering the East End.

On entering the building there will be a lift to bring visitors down into the Undercroft, Treasury and Crypts. Once down below, ramped access throughout the Undercroft will enable smooth access around the museum for everyone. The displays in the Museum will be renewed and some of the many thousands of objects the Minster cares for will be on show in a better way. There will be more and better information about the Minster, its history and its use as a living church today on display in the Undercroft and all around the Minster.

There will also be more and improved toilet facilities for visitors on the north side of the Quire, and more adequate rest areas for staff, volunteers and the Minster Police.

The lighting around the inside of the building will be renewed and made more flexible (and sustainable), and we will be expanding and developing the kinds of educational activities we offer. The YMR Project has also enabled us to take on five apprentice stonemasons in our Works Department and two apprentice glaziers in the York Glaziers' Trust. Through the YMR Project we are continuing the great tradition of stone and glass work that built and maintained great buildings like this one all across Europe.

The whole project will cost about £20 million. There is information about the YMR Project and how you can be involved with the Minster in this work near the displays in the East End.

- There are 14 chapels in York Minster.

- Three are memorial chapels for Yorkshire-based regiments. The Minster itself is the Regimental Chapel of The Yorkshire Regiment.

- The Zouche Chapel, named after Archbishop William de la Zouche, is set aside for private prayer and meditation. The Reserved Sacrament is also kept in here.

- The door in the north wall of the Nave once led through to a chapel called St Sepulchre which, before it was demolished in 1816, was used as stabling for horses with an inn on the upper floor (accessible through a stairway in the buttress outside; the doorway can still be seen).

The Chapels

Before the Reformation there were up to 60 chantry chapels in York Minster.

The Chapels

Like many other cathedrals or large churches, York Minster contains a number of chapels. By the time of the Reformation in the reign of Henry VIII, there were as many as 60. Most of these chapels would have been paid for by wealthy individuals or families, who would also have employed a priest to say a daily Mass for the soul of the departed. These chantry priests lived a communal life in St William's College at the East End of the Minster.

The earliest chapel that exists in the present building is found in the South Transept, and is dedicated to St Michael and All Angels. This is the location of the tomb of Walter de Gray, Archbishop between 1215 and 1255, who established the Chapel of St Michael and All Angels in 1241. The roof boss in the stone vault above his tomb shows St Michael killing the dragon; an image that is reflected on the Purbeck marble effigy of Archbishop de Gray, who is shown forcing the base of his crozier into the dragon's mouth.

With the Reformation the offering of Masses for the departed was stopped, so a great number of these chapels became redundant. The English Civil War and the two disastrous fires of 1829 and 1840 had catastrophic effects on the chapels too, and most have disappeared.

Following the First World War, however, a number of

Left: detail from the reredos in St Stephen's Chapel.
Below: a detail of the Pater Noster altar frontal.

Left: Pater Noster, or Our Father Chapel at the west end of the Nave.
Above: a stained glass window portraying St Christopher carrying Jesus, in St Stephen's Chapel.
Right: Archbishop Toby Mathew in the Lady Chapel.

Yorkshire-based Regiments provided funds to furnish chapels in memory of their soldiers who had given their lives for their country. The first of these regiments was the Duke of Wellington's Regiment in 1923. The chapel is dedicated to All Saints and is found at the east end of the South Quire Aisle. The striking blue velvet altar frontal which incorporates the cap badges of the Regiment was made by the Minster Broderers. On the reredos behind the altar are carved the traditional images of the four evangelists; St Matthew depicted as an angel, St Mark as a winged lion, St Luke as a winged ox and St John as an eagle. In the centre is the Paschal lamb, representing Christ.

Also of interest in this chapel is the latest example of a commissioned piece of painted glass. The lower centre panel in the second window from the east end of the chapel shows the arms of Richard III, a popular king in York. The panel was paid for by the Society of Friends of Richard III, and placed in here in 1997.

At the moment this chapel, along with the other two that are found at the East End; St Stephen's Chapel and the Lady Chapel, have been temporarily taken out of use and are being used for information and displays about the York Minster Revealed Project.

St John's Chapel on the west side of the North Transept

is the Regimental Chapel to the King's Own Yorkshire Light Infantry whose Colonel-in-Chief was the late Queen Mother (d. 2002), and her coat of arms can be seen in the left-hand stained glass window above the altar. In this chapel, just to the right of the entrance, is the tomb of Thomas Haxey, a Treasurer of York Minster. The effigy on top of the tomb is of a cadaver, or corpse, stripped of clothing and in a state of decay, a marked contrast to the effigy of Walter de Gray, who is depicted in his ecclesiastical finery.

St George's Chapel on the west side of the South Transept was the third Regimental Chapel to be created, this time to the Prince of Wales' Own West Yorkshire Regiment.

In this chapel hang the Regimental Colours which, open to the atmosphere, are allowed to 'die'. The kneelers, depicting the cap badge of the Regiment, the white horse and the Prince of Wales' plumage, were made by the Minster Broderers.

The pattern of reinstating chapels after the Great War continued with the creation of St Nicholas' Chapel on the east side of the North Transept. The altar of this chapel is the table tomb of Archbishop Thomas Rotherham who is buried in the Lady Chapel. When the Lady Chapel was renewed there was a desire to move Rotherham's tomb to make space, though his body remains where it was buried.

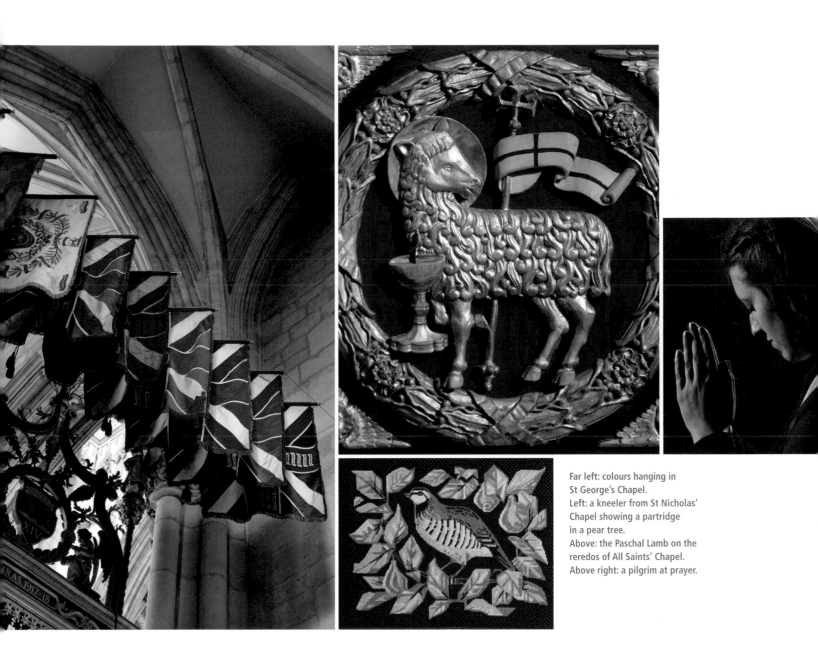

Far left: colours hanging in
St George's Chapel.
Left: a kneeler from St Nicholas'
Chapel showing a partridge
in a pear tree.
Above: the Paschal Lamb on the
reredos of All Saints' Chapel.
Above right: a pilgrim at prayer.

St Nicholas is the patron saint of, among others, children, sailors and pawnbrokers. He is also 'Santa Claus', and for that reason the kneelers show the verses of the song 'The Twelve Days of Christmas'.

Two chapels can be found at the west end of the Nave. On the north side is *Pater Noster*, or the 'Our Father' Chapel. It was created by Dean Milner-White in 1945 as a Chapel where visitors could say the Christian family prayer taught by Jesus; the Lord's Prayer, or 'Our Father'. It has a painting of the Crucifixion by Charles Ricketts (1866–1931).

On the opposite side is the most recent of the chapels, St Cuthbert's. This is the regimental Chapel of the Yorkshire Volunteers, with their crest on the altar frontal. The canopy above was painted by Graeme Wilson and shows St Cuthbert's vision of Heaven, with Christ in Glory and the triumph of good over evil represented by the victory of St George over the dragon, which is seen plummeting from Heaven with Satan.

The chapels of the Minster are used on regular occasions. Each is used on the particular feast day of the saint to whom it is dedicated, and those with military connections are used by the Regiments for their memorial or Association services. St John's Chapel is used on a daily basis for the celebration of Holy Communion at lunchtime.

- York Minster's full name is 'The Cathedral and Metropolitical Church of St Peter in York'.

- York Minster is an Anglican Cathedral.

- The Cathedral is the largest surviving Medieval Gothic cathedral North of the Alps.

- A cathedral is where a bishop has his seat or 'cathedra'.

- A minster, or mynster, was the Anglo-Saxon name for a missionary church.

- York Minster is a church, a cathedral and a minster.

Reference

York Minster is dedicated to St Peter. Symbols representing St Peter include the crossed keys, a cockerel, a church on a rock and an upside-down cross. All of these symbols can be found in the Minster.

Timeline

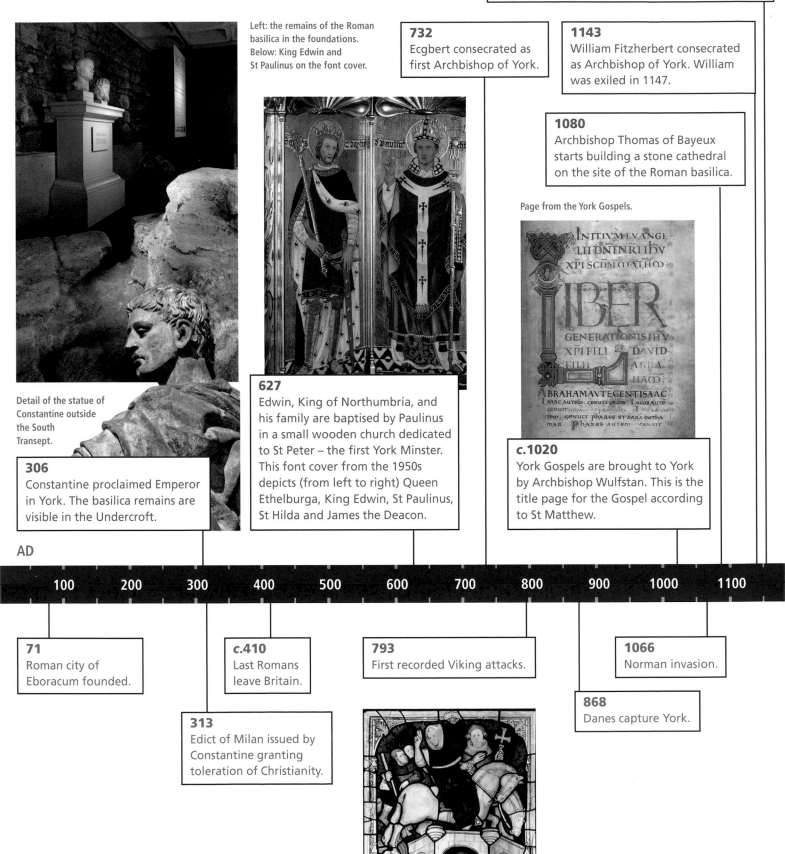

Left: the remains of the Roman basilica in the foundations.
Below: King Edwin and St Paulinus on the font cover.

Detail of the statue of Constantine outside the South Transept.

Page from the York Gospels.

1154
William Fitzherbert returns to York as Archbishop but dies on 8 June from suspected poisoning.

732
Ecgbert consecrated as first Archbishop of York.

1143
William Fitzherbert consecrated as Archbishop of York. William was exiled in 1147.

1080
Archbishop Thomas of Bayeux starts building a stone cathedral on the site of the Roman basilica.

627
Edwin, King of Northumbria, and his family are baptised by Paulinus in a small wooden church dedicated to St Peter – the first York Minster. This font cover from the 1950s depicts (from left to right) Queen Ethelburga, King Edwin, St Paulinus, St Hilda and James the Deacon.

c.1020
York Gospels are brought to York by Archbishop Wulfstan. This is the title page for the Gospel according to St Matthew.

306
Constantine proclaimed Emperor in York. The basilica remains are visible in the Undercroft.

AD

| 100 | 200 | 300 | 400 | 500 | 600 | 700 | 800 | 900 | 1000 | 1100 |

71
Roman city of Eboracum founded.

c.410
Last Romans leave Britain.

793
First recorded Viking attacks.

1066
Norman invasion.

313
Edict of Milan issued by Constantine granting toleration of Christianity.

868
Danes capture York.

St William crossing the River Ouse.

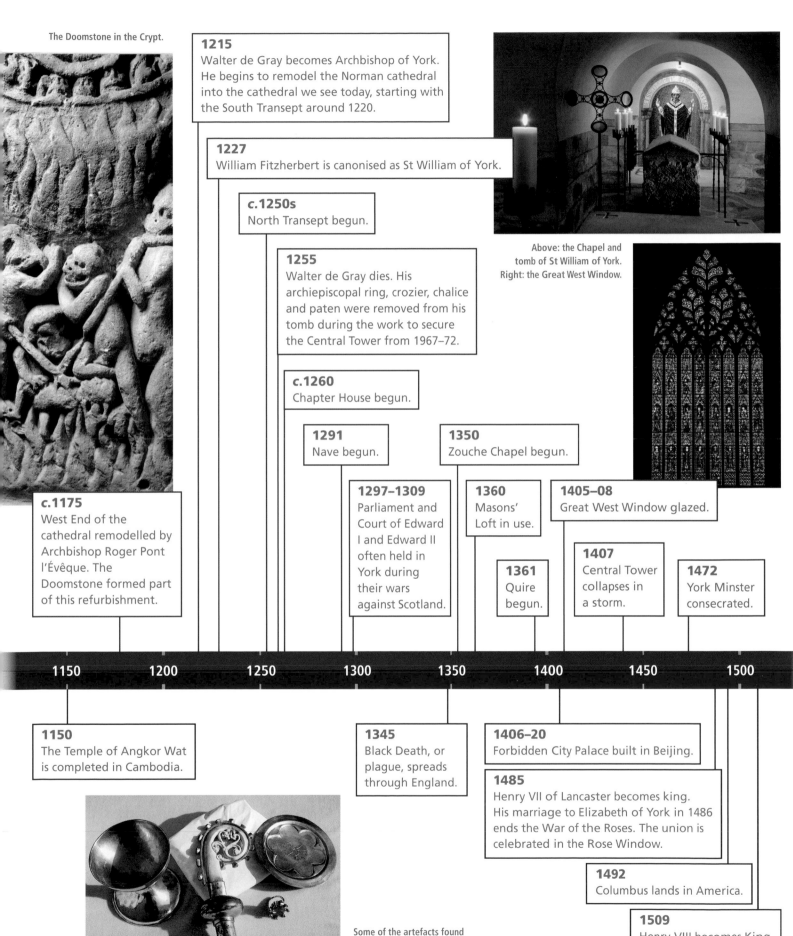

The Doomstone in the Crypt.

1215
Walter de Gray becomes Archbishop of York. He begins to remodel the Norman cathedral into the cathedral we see today, starting with the South Transept around 1220.

1227
William Fitzherbert is canonised as St William of York.

c.1250s
North Transept begun.

1255
Walter de Gray dies. His archiepiscopal ring, crozier, chalice and paten were removed from his tomb during the work to secure the Central Tower from 1967–72.

c.1260
Chapter House begun.

Above: the Chapel and tomb of St William of York.
Right: the Great West Window.

1291
Nave begun.

1350
Zouche Chapel begun.

c.1175
West End of the cathedral remodelled by Archbishop Roger Pont l'Évêque. The Doomstone formed part of this refurbishment.

1297–1309
Parliament and Court of Edward I and Edward II often held in York during their wars against Scotland.

1360
Masons' Loft in use.

1405–08
Great West Window glazed.

1361
Quire begun.

1407
Central Tower collapses in a storm.

1472
York Minster consecrated.

1150   1200   1250   1300   1350   1400   1450   1500

1150
The Temple of Angkor Wat is completed in Cambodia.

1345
Black Death, or plague, spreads through England.

1406–20
Forbidden City Palace built in Beijing.

1485
Henry VII of Lancaster becomes king. His marriage to Elizabeth of York in 1486 ends the War of the Roses. The union is celebrated in the Rose Window.

1492
Columbus lands in America.

Some of the artefacts found with Archbishop de Gray.

1509
Henry VIII becomes King.

The Fairfax memorial
in the Chapter House.

The Nave Sanctuary with
detail of the Burlington floor.

Evensong in the Quire.

1829
Quire destroyed by a
fire started deliberately
by Jonathan Martin.

A concert taking
place in the Nave.

1823
First series of musical
festivities held in the Nave.

1644
Siege of York. York surrenders to the
Parliamentarian forces of Sir Thomas
Fairfax. Fairfax protects the Minster
from damage during this period.

1649
Charles I executed,
making England a
Commonwealth. Dean
and Chapter abolished.

1731
New floor designed and
installed in the Minster
by Lord Burlington and
William Kent.

| 1550 | 1600 | 1650 | 1700 | 1750 | 1800 |

1534
Final breach with Rome
and the formation of the
Church of England.

1642–51
English Civil War.

1660
Restoration of
the Church of
England,
followed by the
Restoration of
the monarchy
through
Charles II in 1661.

1775–83
American War of Independence.

1611
James I issues the
Authorised Version
of the Bible.

1789–99
French
Revolution.

1603
James I becomes king of
both England and Scotland.

A clasp from the King James Version
of the Bible given by King Charles I.

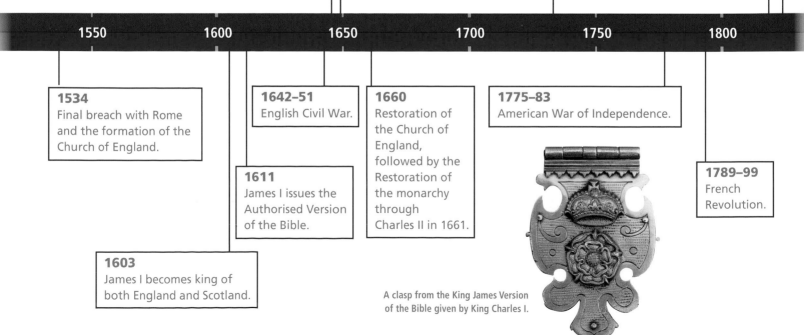

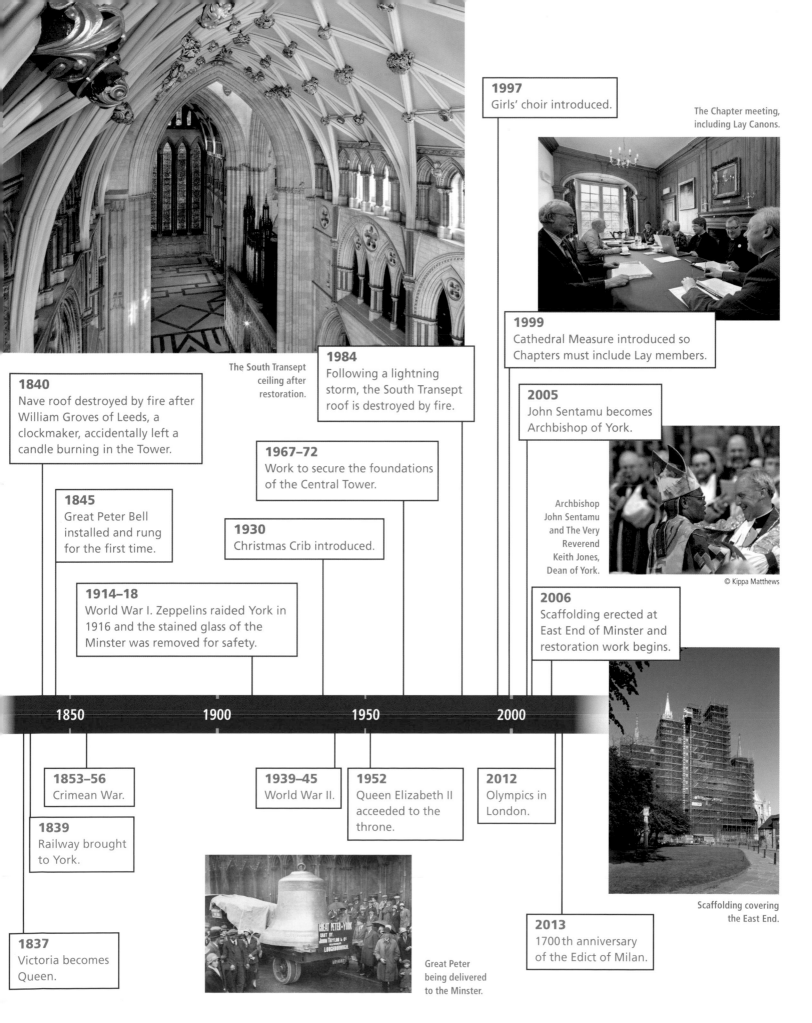

The South Transept ceiling after restoration.

The Chapter meeting, including Lay Canons.

Archbishop John Sentamu and The Very Reverend Keith Jones, Dean of York.

© Kippa Matthews

Scaffolding covering the East End.

Great Peter being delivered to the Minster.

1997
Girls' choir introduced.

1999
Cathedral Measure introduced so Chapters must include Lay members.

2005
John Sentamu becomes Archbishop of York.

2006
Scaffolding erected at East End of Minster and restoration work begins.

1984
Following a lightning storm, the South Transept roof is destroyed by fire.

1840
Nave roof destroyed by fire after William Groves of Leeds, a clockmaker, accidentally left a candle burning in the Tower.

1967–72
Work to secure the foundations of the Central Tower.

1845
Great Peter Bell installed and rung for the first time.

1930
Christmas Crib introduced.

1914–18
World War I. Zeppelins raided York in 1916 and the stained glass of the Minster was removed for safety.

1850   1900   1950   2000

1853–56
Crimean War.

1939–45
World War II.

1952
Queen Elizabeth II acceded to the throne.

2012
Olympics in London.

1839
Railway brought to York.

1837
Victoria becomes Queen.

2013
1700th anniversary of the Edict of Milan.

Glossary

Advent / Advent Wreath The 4-week period leading up to Christmas; a time of preparation. Five candles in the Advent Wreath to remember important people and prepare for the birth of Jesus.

Altar The table on which Christians celebrate the meal of bread and wine to remember Jesus.

Arcade An arcade is a succession of arches, each supported by columns; a 'blind arcade' is arcading against a solid wall.

Archbishop The most senior leader in the Church of England's two provinces, Canterbury and York. The Archbishop of York is Dr John Sentamu.

Bible Holy book made up of two parts for Christians: the Old Testament or the Hebrew Bible, and the New Testament. Christians and Jews share a reverence for the Hebrew Bible.

Broderers The skilled volunteers who embroider cloth and make vestments for use in York Minster.

Cathedra / Cathedral From the Latin for 'chair' or the Greek for 'seat'; the cathedra is the chair or throne of a bishop and the symbol of his or her teaching authority. A cathedral is a church where the bishop has his or her seat.

Chantry Term for a fund established to pay for a priest to celebrate sung Masses for the soul of the deceased donor. A chantry chapel is a dedicated area within a greater church, set aside or built especially for and dedicated to the performance of the chantry duties.

Chapter (Dean and Chapter) The body of people responsible for a cathedral. In York it is made up of a Dean and four ordained canons and three lay canons; they meet monthly.

Chapter House A building or room attached to a cathedral or collegiate church in which meetings are held.

Church A gathering place for Christians for worship, social activity and service to the community; not always a building built for the purpose. Some meet in halls or schools. They are about the people who meet in them: the people are the church.

Church Year / Season Church year begins with Advent Sunday (end Nov.) and moves through Christmas, Lent, Easter, Pentecost and Trinity. See www.yorkminster.org for more information.

Coat of Arms A symbol unique to a person, family, corporation or state; like a personal 'logo'.

College of Canons Clergy and Lay people who are canons but do not work in the cathedral; in York the College is made up of 44 members.

Commonwealth The time between the execution of Charles I and the Restoration of the monarchy under Charles II; usually about 1649–58.

Cope A liturgical vestment; a very long cloak, open in front and fastened at the breast with a band or clasp.

Clerestory The upper part of the nave, choir, and transepts of a large church, containing a series of windows. It is clear of the roofs of the aisles and admits light to the central parts of the building.

Cross The main symbol of the Christian faith; Jesus was killed by crucifixion by the Romans. A cross with an image of Jesus on it is called a crucifix.

Crozier Shaped like a shepherd's crook. A bishop carries this staff as 'shepherd of the flock of God'.

Crypt A stone chamber or vault beneath the floor of a church usually used as a chapel or burial vault.

Easter The day when Christians celebrate Jesus rising from the dead; the season following Easter until Pentecost in the Church's year.

Ecclesiastical Of or relating to the Christian Church; from the Greek word used for the Church, *ekklesia*.

Effigy A representation of a person, especially in the form of sculpture or some other three-dimensional form.

English Civil War A series of armed conflicts between Parliamentarians (Roundheads) and Royalists (Cavaliers).The series of wars (1642–51) saw fighting between supporters of the King and supporters of Parliament. The Civil War ended with the Parliamentary victory at the battle of Worcester on 3 September 1651. (See also 'Restoration' below.)

Evangelists The writers of the four Gospels in the New Testament part of the Bible: Matthew, Mark, Luke and John. From the Greek word for 'gospel' or 'good news'.

Evensong A choral version of the Church of England's service of Evening Prayer; usually said or sung in the late afternoon or early evening.

Feast / Feast Day A day when the life, death or memory of a saint is honoured in the Church; it is a break from the routine (hence a 'feast') and is meant to strengthen or nurture faith.

Font An article of church furniture used for holding water for baptism; baptism is the ceremony through which people become members of the Church.

Frieze A long stretch of painted or sculpted decoration normally above eye level.

Frontal A drapery covering the front of an altar.

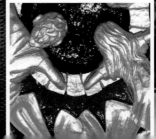

Left to right: detail of the Coat of arms of John Eyre in the North Quire Aisle; the symbol of St John the Evangelist created by a Minster Broderer; detail of a South Transept boss; details of the Norman columns in the Crypt.

Gilded A number of decorative techniques for applying fine gold leaf or powder to solid surfaces such as wood, stone, or metal to give a thin coating of gold. A gilded object is described as 'gilt'.

Good Friday The day on which Jesus was crucified. It is called 'good' because Christians believe that his death brings salvation and a new relationship to God and so is good for humankind.

Gothic Originating in 12th-century France and lasting into the 16th century, its characteristic features include the pointed arch, the ribbed vault and the flying buttress.

Lent The 40-day period leading up to Easter; a time used to prepare for the death of Jesus on Good Friday and his Resurrection on Easter Day, traditionally through acts of service to others and self-denial.

Mason A person who works stone to create simple or complex designs to make a building or other structure.

Mass / Holy Communion The service in Christian churches where Christians recall the life and death of Jesus and his last meal with his disciples through sharing bread and wine.

Niche A space in a wall where a statue or other carving might be placed.

Papal Tiara The three-tiered papal crown.

Paschal Lamb Refers to the way in which for Christians Jesus' death is seen as a sacrifice; he is called the 'Lamb of God' in the New Testament; refers also to the Passover Lamb (from *Pascha* the Latin for Passover).

Patron Saint A saint who is seen as one who prays in heaven for a nation, place, craft, activity, class, clan, family, or person. St Andrew is the Patron Saint of Scotland, St George of England, St David of Wales and St Patrick of Ireland.

Peter One of the first followers of of Jesus. He was a fisherman, seen by some as the first Bishop of Rome, Patron saint of York Minster.

Pilgrimage A journey or search of moral or spiritual significance. Many religions see pilgrimage as important.

Plantagenet Royal family which ruled England from 1154 until 1485.

Primatial / Primate In the Church of England, a Primate is an archbishop of a province (called a 'primatial see') which confers precedence over other bishops. The Archbishop of York is Primate of England.

Quire An ancient spelling of 'choir' used to distinguish the space from the group that sings in it.

Reformation A period of religious upheaval in Europe during which a number of theologians protested against the Roman Catholic Church and formed new churches including the Church of England, the Lutheran and Reformed Churches. The most common dating begins in 1517 when Luther published the '95 Theses' and concludes in 1648.

Relic / Reliquary A relic is an object or a personal item of religious significance, carefully preserved as a physical memorial of a person or an event. A reliquary is a special container for a relic.

Reredos A screen or decoration behind the altar in a church showing religious images; also called an altarpiece.

Restoration The Restoration of the monarchy began in 1660 when the English, Scottish and Irish monarchies were all restored under Charles II after the English Civil War and the Commonwealth.

Roof Boss The carved underside of the key (stone or wood) that forms the meeting point of several converging vaulting ribs to hold them together and in place.

Saint A holy person. For Christians a 'saint' is any believer who is 'in Christ'.

Salvation For Christians this has two main parts: being freed from sin and guilt and having a new relationship to God through the life, death and resurrection of Jesus Christ. See www.yorkminster.org for more information.

Sill The bottom horizontal part of a wall or building to which vertical parts are attached.

Tracery The stonework elements that support the glass in a Gothic window. The term probably derives from the 'tracing floors' on which the patterns of late Gothic windows were laid out, such as the Minster's Masons' Loft.

Transept A section of any building, which lies across the main body of the building; in Christian churches, a transept is an area set across the nave to form the shape of a cross.

Triforium A gallery forming an upper storey to the aisle of a church and typically an arcaded storey between the nave arches and clerestory.

Tudor The royal house of Welsh origin that ruled England from 1485 until 1603.

Verger Men and women responsible for the order and upkeep of the church, its furnishings and preparations for worship. Named after the staff of the office, from the Latin *virga* meaning 'twig' or 'rod'.

Vestibule A lobby, entrance hall, or passage between an outer door and the interior of a building.

Vestry A vestry is a room in or attached to a church in which the vestments, vessels, records, etc., are kept, and in which the clergy and choir dress for services.

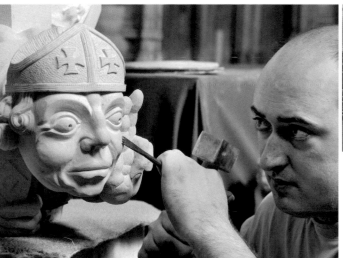

Left to right; the Crucifix in the South Transept; Matthew Hodgkinson working stone; detail from the moveable font.

Further Information

Opening Times

Daily for early services from 7.00 am.
For sightseeing: Mon–Sat: 9.00 am
(9.30 am November-March) – last entry 5.30 pm.
Sunday: 12.00 noon–3.45 pm.
Opening times may change subject
to major cathedral services;
please check in advance of your visit
to avoid disappointment.

Service Times

Mon–Sat: 7.30 am; 7.45 am; 12.30 pm; 5.15 pm.
Sunday: 8.00 am; 10.00 am; 11.30 am; 4.00 pm.

Admission

Charges apply for the Minster and Undercroft,
and a separate charge for the Tower.

Guided tours are offered free of charge by our team
of voluntary guides (when available).

Shop

The Minster has two main shops, one located off the Nave
and the other just outside the Minster in Minster Gates.
They sell a wide range of souvenir and gift items,
many based on, or inspired by, the Minster and its
collections. You can also visit our on-line shop via the
Minster's website.

School Visits

To find out about bringing school parties to the Minster,
call the Centre for School Visits –
tel: 0844 939 0017 or email: schoolvisits@yorkminster.org.

Group Bookings

Can be arranged by contacting the Visitors' Department –
tel: 0844 939 0011 or email: groups@yorkminster.org.

Conferences and Events

York Minster is a magnificent venue for a wide range of
events from concerts and lectures to fine dining and
corporate hospitality. To find out more –
tel: 0844 939 0015 or email: events@yorkminster.org.

Disabled Access

Ground Level and Precincts

A permanent stone ramp has been constructed at the
West End of the Minster. A temporary ramp is in place
outside the south door. Inside, there is a ramp from the
Nave into the Quire and from the North Transept to the
Chapter House.

Assistance dogs are welcomed at the Minster.
Wheelchairs for use in the Minster are available on request.
Toilet facilities are available for use by disabled visitors.

Further Information

York Minster, Church House, Ogleforth, York YO1 7JN
tel: 0844 939 0011
email: info@yorkminster.org
website: www.yorkminster.org

© The Dean and Chapter of York and Jigsaw Design & Publishing.
Text by York Minster.
Photographs by Peter Smith of Newbery Smith Photography Ltd,
York Minster and York Glaziers' Trust.
ISBN 978-1-907750-29-8
Designed and produced by Jigsaw Design & Publishing.
Printed in Great Britain 10137-1/11

Use this QR code for further information.